Pebble® Plus

Creepy Crawlers

Scorpions

by Esther Porter

Gail Saunders-Smith, PhD, Consulting Editor

Consultant: Wade Harrell
Vice President
American Tarantula Society

CAPSTONE PRESS
a capstone imprint

Pebble Plus is published by Capstone Press,
1710 Roe Crest Drive, North Mankato, Minnesota 56003.
www.capstonepub.com

Library of Congress Cataloging-in-Publication Data
Porter, Esther.
Scorpions / by Esther Porter.
p. cm.—(Pebble Plus. Creepy Crawlers)
Summary: "Learn about scorpions, including how and where they live and how these creepy creatures are important
parts of their world"—Provided by publisher.
Audience: 005-008.
Audience: K to grade 3.
Includes bibliographical references and index.
ISBN 978-1-4765-2064-3 (library binding)
ISBN 978-1-4765-3479-4 (eBook PDF)
1. Scorpions—Juvenile literature. I. Title.
QL458.7.P67 2014
595.4'6—dc23   2013005524

Editorial Credits
Jeni Wittrock, editor; Kyle Grenz, designer; Laura Manthe, production specialist

Photo Credits
Alamy: WILDLIFE GmbH, 5; Chad Campbell, 17; James P. Rowan, 11; Minden Pictures: Foto Natura/James Christensen, 15;
National Geographic Stock: Carsten Peter, 9; Newscom: Ivan Kuzmin Image Broker, 19; Shutterstock: Arnoud Quanjer, 21;
Audrey Snider-Bell, 7, cover, Dave Rock, 13, paulrommer, 1, vlastas66, design element (throughout)

Note to Parents and Teachers

The Creepy Crawlers set supports national science standards related to life science. This book
describes and illustrates scorpions. The images support early readers in understanding the text. The
repetition of words and phrases helps early readers learn new words. This book also introduces
early readers to subject-specific vocabulary words, which are defined in the Glossary section. Early
readers may need assistance to read some words and to use the Table of Contents, Glossary, Read
More, Internet Sites, and Index sections of the book.

Printed in China by Nordica.
0413/CA21300494
032013   007226NORDF13

Table of Contents

Secret Creeper

In secret, unseen places,

scorpions hide. If you bother

a scorpion, watch out!

These creepy crawlers

can pinch and sting.

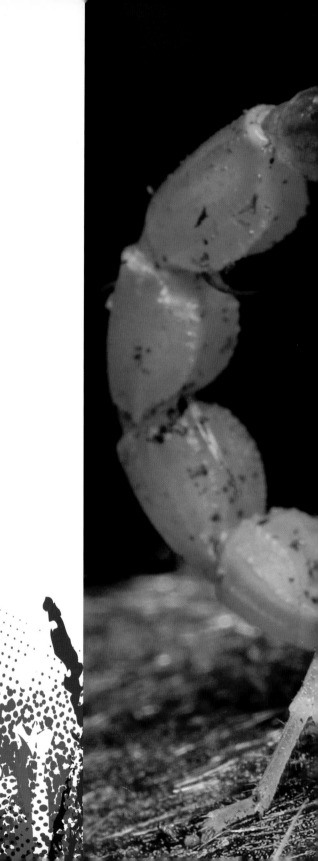

There are more than 1,500 kinds
of scorpions. These arachnids
can be 0.5 inch (1.3 centimeters)
to 8 inches (20 cm) long.

Creature of the Night

Scorpions are nocturnal. During the day, they hide in cracks and burrows or under logs and rocks. They live in all but the coldest places.

Scorpions have up to 12 eyes. Two eyes are big. The rest are small. Scorpions cannot see well, but they see best in dim light.

eyes

Scorpions can't see well, but they feel everything around them. Tiny hairs on scorpions' bodies sense what is nearby.

Waiting Game

A scorpion sits quietly, waiting for prey to pass by. A cricket gets close. The scorpion grabs its food with its pincers.

The scorpion stings its prey with a barb at the end of its body. The sting contains venom. This poison turns the prey's insides to mush.

barb

Lives of Scorpions

A female scorpion gives birth to between 8 and 30 babies. The scorplings ride on her back for a few weeks. Then the young scorpions hunt on their own.

Most scorpions grow quickly
and live from 2 to 25 years.
No matter the age, scorpions
share one more creepy feature.
Under a black light, they glow!

Glossary

arachnid—a group of animals that includes spiders, scorpions, mites, and ticks

barb—the clawlike part at the end of a scorpion's body that stings its prey and its enemies

black light—a lightbulb that shines blue-black light; scorpions glow under black lights

pincer—a lobsterlike claw used to grab and pinch

prey—an animal hunted by another animal for food

nocturnal—active at night

scorpling—a baby scorpion

sense—to feel

venom—a liquid poison made by an animal to kill its prey

Read More

Bodden, Valerie. *Scorpions*. Creepy Creatures. Mankato, Minn.: Creative Education, 2011.

Ganeri, Anita. *Scorpion*. A Day in the Life. Desert Animals. Chicago: Heinemann Library, 2011.

Gonzales, Doreen. *Scorpions in the Dark*. Creatures of the Night. New York: PowerKids Press, 2010.

Internet Sites

FactHound offers a safe, fun way to find Internet sites related to this book. All of the sites on FactHound have been researched by our staff.

Here's all you do:

Visit *www.facthound.com*

Type in this code: 9781476520643

Super-cool stuff! Check out projects, games and lots more at
www.capstonekids.com

Index

Word Count: 215
Grade: 1
Early-Intervention Level: 19